LET'S VISIT THE VATICAN

Let's visit the VATICAN

KIERAN CONRY

ACKNOWLEDGEMENTS

The Author and Publishers are grateful to the following organizations and individuals for permission to reproduce copyright photographs in this book:

E.N.I.T.—London; Chris Fairclough; International Photobank; The Mansell Collection; and Ronald Sheridan's Photo Library.

CIP data
Conry, Kieran
   Let's visit the Vatican
   1.   Vatican City – Social life and customs – Juvenile literature
   I.   Title
   954'.634   DG800
   ISBN 0 222 01009 6
Burke Publishing Company Limited
Pegasus House, 116–120 Golden Lane, London EC1Y 0TL, England.
Burke Publishing (Canada) Limited
Registered Office: 20 Queen Street West, Suite 3000, Box 30, Toronto, Canada M5H 1V5.
Burke Publishing Company Inc.
Registered Office: 333 State Street, PO Box 1740, Bridgeport, Connecticut 06601, U.S.A.
Filmset in "Monophoto" Baskerville by Green Gates Studios Ltd., Hull, England.
Printed in Singapore by Tien Wah Press (Pte.) Ltd.

Contents

THE VATICAN

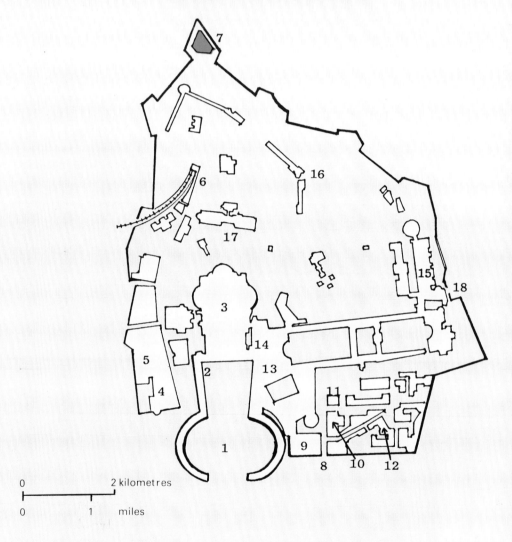

0 _____ 2 kilometres

0 _____ 1 _____ miles

1. St. Peter's Square
2. The Arch of the Bells
3. St. Peter's Basilica
4. Palace of the Holy Office
5. Audience Hall
6. Vatican Railway Station
7. Helipad
8. Porta Sant'Anna
9. Swiss Guard Barracks
10. Printing Press
11. Post Office
12. *L'Osservatore Romano* Offices
13. Apostolic Palace
14. Sistine Chapel
15. Vatican Museums
16. Vatican Radio
17. Palace of Vatican City Government
18. Entrance to Museums

The City of Rome and the Early Christian Church

The Vatican is a state within a city. Geographically, it is part of the city of Rome, but it is also an independent state with its own laws and institutions. In order to understand and appreciate the position of the Vatican in the world today, we must go back and look at its history. However, because of its geographical location within the city of Rome, any account of the history of the Vatican must include an account of the history of Rome. This will also help us to understand the relationship between the city of Rome and the Vatican state.

Rome is supposed to get its name from Romulus, one of the legendary founders of the city. According to the legend, the twin babies Romulus and Remus were cast into the River Tiber by their wicked great-uncle who had seized the throne of the kingdom of Alba from his own brother. Miraculously, they did not drown but were washed ashore and found by a she-wolf who fed them on her own milk. In the course of time, they restored their grandfather to the throne, killed their great-uncle, and went on to found a city on the site where they had been washed ashore. The image of the two babies being fed by the she-wolf can still be seen everywhere in Rome today, for it is the symbol of the city.

It is difficult to separate fact from legend, of course, but we

St. Peter's Basilica—
the most famous
building in the Vatican
City State

can say with reasonable certainty that a settlement was established some time in the second half of the eighth century B.C. (before Christ) by people from the plain of Latium on the western side of the central part of Italy.

The first settlement was on a hill called the Palatine, which is one of a group of seven hills on the south bank of the River Tiber. The Palatine is joined to another hill near by called the Esquiline. This natural fortress, with the river to the north of it, formed an effective defence against the Etruscan tribes to the north.

The Sabines, a tribe from the same region of Latium, occupied a third hill, called the Capitol.

Gradually the other hills in the area (hills of hardened volcanic lava—it should be remembered that Italy still has at least one active volcano, Etna) were also settled. The area between and below them, an uninhabitable swamp, was drained and became the site of a market place—this was to become the Roman Forum.

Tradition says that there were seven successive kings of this increasingly powerful city. The last of the kings, Tarquin, was expelled in about 509 B.C. and the Republic of Rome came into being. The Republic of Rome rapidly expanded through what we now know as the Italian peninsula and into North Africa. It then spread west into the Iberian peninsula, east through Greece into Asia Minor and into the Egyptian Empire.

At the time of the birth of Christ, the Roman Empire had spread beyond the Alps as far as the Rhine and the Danube. A little later it was also to establish itself to the west, in Britain. On its most eastern border was the province of Palestine, which included the tiny village of Bethlehem.

Jesus Christ was born shortly before the Roman Empire reached the peak of its power. The first people to spread the message of Christ were the members of the small band of disciples who had followed Jesus during his lifetime. Jesus had lived and died near Jerusalem, yet within a very few years his followers were to take his teaching far beyond the confines of Palestine.

St. Matthew's gospel tells us how on one occasion Jesus asked his disciples who they thought he was. Only one of the disciples was able to give a definite and confident answer. This man declared that Jesus was the Christ, the Son of the living God. Jesus then said to him " . . thou art Peter, and upon this rock I will build my church".

Peter was therefore chosen by Christ as the man who was to

The ruins of the ancient Roman Forum, with the Colosseum (left) and the Arch of Titus (right) in the background

become the foundation of the Christian Church; and after the death of Christ and his resurrection, Peter was accepted as the head of the small group of apostles. (The name Peter in Greek means "rock").

But why did Jerusalem not become the centre of Christianity? After all, Jesus died in Jerusalem and it was there that the apostles first began to tell people about him.

To answer this question, we must take a brief look at the history of Palestine.

The Romans had captured Jerusalem sixty-four years before the birth of Christ, and ever since then Palestine had been a source of trouble for them. Things came to a head in A.D. 64 (A.D. means "the year of the Lord", since we measure our years from the birth of Christ), when there was an open revolt. The Romans began a four-year siege of Jerusalem; and the Temple, the great symbol of Jewish power, was finally destroyed by the Roman Emperor Titus. All that was left standing was what is now called the "Wailing Wall". The Jews were scattered throughout the world.

If the Christian Church was to survive, it had to become independent of Jerusalem, move away from it, and spread the message of Christ to all people throughout the known world. By this time, Peter—the leader of the apostles, and the man chosen by Christ to become the foundation of the Christian Church—was already in Rome; and it seemed that Rome, the capital of the empire in which Christianity had come into existence, was the place from which it could be most effective.

11

Below the hills or ridges on which the first settlers made their home, the River Tiber bends in a broad loop. Inside the loop is the area known as the *Campus Martius*, the "Field of Mars". It was originally an open space for exercise and drill. On the other side of the loop there is another small hill in an area that was known in Roman times as the *Ager Vaticanus*. The word *ager* also means "field", and this was an area of villas and gardens across the river, away from the bustle of the city itself. It is not quite clear where the name *Vaticanus* comes from.

Here, too, was the Circus of Nero—not a circus in our sense

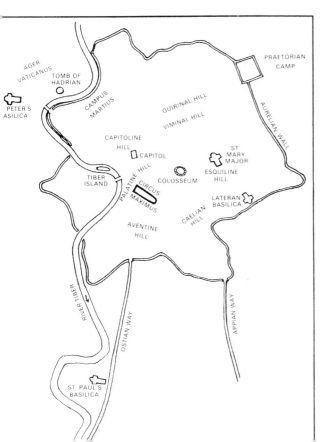

Map of Imperial Rome

The Arch of Titus, erected to commemorate the destruction of Jerusalem by the Emperor Titus in A.D. 68. Inside the arch are carvings showing the Roman soldiers carrying the famous seven-branched candlesticks away from the Temple

of the word, but a stadium for races. It was here that the first of the great persecutions of the Christians came to a climax, when the Emperor Nero had countless Christians put to a horrible death. He is said to have made human torches of some of them. This was between A.D. 64 and 67, after the fire of Rome. It is not known how many Christians died at this time, or whether Nero actually tried to blame them for the fire, but what is fairly certain is that during this persecution, St. Peter was put to death. It seems that, having died in the stadium on

13

The Colosseum, or Flavian Amphitheatre, completed towards the end of the first century A.D. The persecutions of the early Christians took place in amphitheatres such as this one

the Vatican Hill, St. Peter was then buried in the nearby cemetery.

What is important for us is not so much the precise date of St. Peter's death as the place, and the site of his burial; for it is from this that what we know today as the Vatican takes its name.

14

The Tomb of the Apostle Peter

Because of the important position which Peter held in the early Church, his burial place quickly became a centre for Christian devotion. During another persecution, the body may have been moved to one of the "catacombs" (the underground cemeteries outside Rome) for safe keeping, but this would not have been for long. The tomb of St. Peter was on the Vatican Hill.

Initially, the tomb was marked with a small memorial building in the style common to many of the more important Roman graves. The memorial was a fairly simple brick building. The plaster on its inside walls was covered with "graffiti"— messages left by the faithful who came to pray at the tomb. Among the names that were carved there were the names of Christ, Mary and Peter himself.

At this stage, Christianity was still not generally accepted, but when Constantine was declared Emperor of Rome in 306, he took a decision that was to have the most important, lasting consequences both for the Christian Church and for Rome itself: he declared that Christianity would, from then on, be tolerated within the Roman Empire. One of the most important results of Constantine's generally favourable attitude towards the Christian Church was that the Church and the State were now much closer; and as Rome was the capital of the Empire (or the western half of it, at least), the power of the Bishop of Rome increased accordingly.

Constantine made a great contribution to the history of the Church and also left many lasting memorials of his rule. One of the most important memorials was the basilica which he ordered to be built over the tomb of St. Peter. Constantine had ordered that the memorial to St. Peter (at this stage only a simple brick building) should be covered with a shrine built of marble and porphyry (a semi-precious red stone), open at one side to allow access to the tomb. Constantine then erected a huge basilica around this—a fitting monument to the first Bishop of Rome, the man whom Christ himself had chosen as the one to lead the Church.

This great church remained for over a thousand years until it was replaced by the present Basilica of St. Peter, which was begun in 1506 and blessed on 18th November 1626.

In 1940, Pope Pius XII ordered that excavation work should be carried out under the High Altar in St. Peter's Basilica. This was an attempt to discover what was there, and how much truth there was in the story that the bones of the Apostle lay under the altar where the Pope, the modern successor of St. Peter, says mass.

These excavations showed that there was indeed a tomb under the High Altar, and that it contained human bones. The bones were of one man, a powerfully-built man (Peter had been a fisherman, remember) who had been fairly old when he died (work it out: Jesus had died some thirty years before him at the

16

The present Basilica of St. Peter

age of thirty-three or so). There were also traces of cloth, purple in colour with threads of gold—another sign that this was the tomb of an important man.

All this seems to indicate that the tomb under the High Altar is indeed the tomb of the man whom we refer to today as St. Peter. This is the reason why the Vatican is where it is. It is the site of the burial place of St. Peter. The Roman Catholic Church, whose highest authority is the Pope in Rome, is still referred to as the See (the throne) of Peter; and the Pope is regarded as Peter's successor.

The Collapse of the Roman Empire

It is misleading at this early stage to talk of "The Vatican" in the way that we do today, for to begin with it was not even the site of the residence of the popes. The first official papal residence that we might compare with the Vatican was the Lateran palace. This was given to the Church by the Emperor Constantine. It was built on land that had formerly belonged to the Laterani family but which had been confiscated by the state under the Emperor Nero.

The Arch of Constantine, built in A.D. 315. Many of the pieces of stone used in its construction were taken from earlier monuments

The statue of the Emperor Marcus Aurelius on the Capitol Hill. For a long time it was thought that the figure on the horse was Constantine; this probably saved the statue from being melted down

To see what happened to Peter's successors we must look at the history of Rome, for the histories of the papacy and the city of Rome cannot be separated.

In A.D. 330 the Emperor Constantine took a decision which was to have profound consequences. He made the old city of Byzantium, on the Bosphorus (the strait that links the Black Sea with the Aegean and Mediterranean) the new capital of the Roman Empire. It was renamed after him, and became Constantinople.

The western half of the empire had begun to decline, while the eastern half was becoming more prosperous. The empire was also by now too big to administer from Rome, and so, inevitably, power shifted to the east.

The east also appeared more secure because of what was now happening on the northern borders of the empire, on the other side of the Danube and the Rhine.

The furthest limits of the empire in the west, especially the provinces of Britain and Gaul, had begun to suffer serious social upheaval. They were becoming more expensive to garrison and to administer and were becoming less productive: agriculture went into decline and the population began to dwindle.

Over the borders, ready to move in and benefit from the now unstable and insecure state of these northern parts of the empire, were the barbarian tribes.

Britain came under attack from Picts and Scots in the north and from Angles, Saxons and Jutes from the mainland. It was finally abandoned by the Romans in the year 407.

Just north of the Danube were the Visigoths under their leader, Alaric. He was allowed to settle peacefully south of the Danube, but then saw the opportunity to gain even more land by invading Italy. At first he got no further than Lombardy in the north. The Visigoths were paid to turn back.

But they were not kept out for long. In the year 410 Alaric besieged and finally sacked Rome, and for three days his soldiers pillaged the city. It is a mistake to regard all the barbarian tribes as pagans: Alaric had been converted to a type of Christ-

A battle between Romans and barbarian tribesmen as depicted on a sarcophagus now in a Rome museum

ianity and in fact the churches in Rome were spared. For the Roman Empire, however, it was really the end.

Another barbarian tribe, the Vandals (a name which we do not now immediately associate with this period of history), moved south from the area between the Rivers Vistula and Elbe in the north of Europe. Passing through Gaul they occupied Spain, and from there could conquer the province of North Africa. In A.D. 455 they landed at the Roman port of Ostia before moving on the city itself. When they finally left, the people were grateful that the city had not been burned; but they had little else to be grateful for, except their lives. The troops of Alaric had spent three days plundering Rome: the Vandals pillaged for two weeks.

But before them had come the Huns, under the famous Attila. They invaded Italy from the north, halting at Mantua. There Attila had a personal meeting with someone who had come to plead with him on behalf of the city and people of Rome. Attila may have decided already, as a result of disease and hunger in his army, not to advance as far as Rome, but this is not so important. What is of greater interest is the fact that the man who came to talk with him was not the Emperor, or even a soldier. He was Pope Leo I, otherwise known as Leo the Great.

The Growth of Papal Power

Constantine had offered many privileges to the Christian Church—besides his generosity to Christian shrines in Rome and the Holy Land, he brought in many laws favourable to the clergy. He also made Sunday a public holiday. With the new power that Constantine gave it, the Church began to organise itself along the lines on which the empire had been run.

Like the empire, the Christian Church was divided into large provinces: the head of each church "province" was a "Patriarch", having authority over the bishops in the cities within the area. The were five great Patriarchs: in Jerusalem (for obvious reasons), Alexandria in Egypt, Antioch in Asia Minor, the new capital of Constantinople, and Rome. (It will be noted that four of these five "Patriarchates" were in the eastern half of the empire: only Rome belonged to the west).

After the division of the empire, there was to be a serious problem over the question of authority in the Church at large; and this came to a head over the debate about what was to be said of Christ. In the west it was recognized that Christ is one person who is, at the same time, both fully God and fully man. In the east, however, a number of ideas quite different from this (for example, that Christ was either only God or only man, but not both) were put forward as the belief of the Church.

The empire had been split, and now the Church was to follow its example. In the debates about the person of Christ, Rome claimed to have ultimate authority to make decisions about matters of faith, since it had the authority of the apostles, which could be traced back to Christ himself.

The Patriarchs in the east, however, rejected the claims of Rome; and this was the beginning of a split between the Christian Church of the west (the Roman or "Latin" Church) and the Christian Church in the east (the "Orthodox" Church) which was made final in 1054 and which is still very real today.

The cause of the split (or "Schism", as it is called) is especially interesting, since now we see Rome making a particular and strong claim to a special position as a teaching authority in the Church, higher than any other, and basing the claim on the fact that its bishop is the successor of the Apostle Peter.

It is for this, rather than his meeting with Attila, that Leo I is called Great, for he was the first pope to make this claim openly. He said in the sermon which he gave at his coronation

23

The statue of St. Peter, in the Basilica dedicated to his memory

that he was not just one bishop among many. He spoke of St. Peter, as "the Blessed Apostle Peter, in whose chair his power lives on,"—and of course Leo was now sitting in that chair. From now on the Bishop of Rome would claim to speak with the authority of Christ himself. Leo took to himself a title that had previously belonged to the Emperor, that of *Pontifex Maximus*. It is a title that is still used today by the Pope, the "Supreme Pontiff".

24

The Middle Ages and the Papal States

It is difficult to say precisely when the period of history which we call the Middle Ages began. It is equally difficult to give a precise date for the beginning of the growth of the political power of the Pope. During the Middle Ages, however, the Pope became a very powerful political leader, the ruler of vast territories known as the Papal States.

An influential figure in the rise of the Papal States was Pope Gregory I. He organized the defence of Rome and of many cities to which he appointed governors. He also saw to the administration of the land and properties that had been left to the Church—particularly in Italy, but also in Spain, Africa, Gaul and the East. Much of Sicily, too, came under direct papal rule: the Church was the biggest single land-owner in Italy.

However, these papal possessions (which provided important revenue for the upkeep of Rome and much else that was of great benefit to the people) were now threatened by invasion from the Lombards. In 751 the Lombards marched on Rome. Pope Stephen II turned for help north of the Alps, to the Franks. Their King, Pepin, welcomed him and made an alliance with him. Pepin guaranteed to protect the territories of the Pope, and in return Stephen consecrated Pepin as king of the Franks.

This alliance did save Rome and Italy from the Lombards and, under the protection of the Franks, the Pope now ruled much of Italy. By this time, the Pope had great political power.

This situation was confirmed by Pepin's son, Charlemagne, who came to Rome in 800 and was crowned in that year, on

The coronation of Charlemagne in A.D. 800—a stained-glass window in Strasbourg Cathedral (France)

Christmas Day, as "the greatest peace-bringing Emperor of the Romans". The west was an empire again, this time a Christian one, and the Pope's authority, both spiritual and territorial, was secure.

The eleventh century, however, was a black period in the history of the popes. Pope John XI died of poison. John XII was deposed by the Emperor and another Pope, Leo VIII, put in his place. Fighting between rival groups in Rome was common at the time, and the chair of Peter had a number of occupants as one party or another gained the upper hand.

Worse was to come, however: Benedict IX was so corrupt that he was chased from Rome and a rival, Sylvester III, put on the papal throne. Attempting to benefit as much as possible from the situation, Benedict sold the papacy! So that when he later tried to re-claim his papal title, there were three men using the title "Pope".

Temporary reform came with Pope Gregory V, the first German pope, whose appointment was secured by the Emperor Otto III. He was appalled by what was happening in Rome, as were many of the bishops in Germany and France. "This is not the papacy!" the French bishops complained.

It was not until the papacy of Leo IX, however, between 1049 and 1054, that a period of true and lasting reform began. Leo IX was elected not in Rome, but in the court of the Emperor Henry III in Worms, in Germany. After the election made it clear that he had been chosen unanimously, Leo asked for three days to fast and pray before deciding whether to accept or not. In the end he agreed, on condition that the clergy and people of Rome accepted him as their spiritual leader. This was a return to the true spirit of the role of the Pope and the beginning of real reform.

It was with the reign of Pope Innocent III that the papacy reached the peak of its power. In 1215 Innocent III summoned a meeting of bishops and other important people in the Church, from all over the world, and over two thousand gathered in the Lateran (still today the official papal residence). This became known as the Lateran Council, and was concerned with stopping the spread of heresy and improving standards of education among the clergy and people.

Shortly before this, Innocent III, one of the most powerful men in Europe, met one of the most humble and simple. The man came from a small village north of Rome, and he wanted the Pope to give his approval to a community he had founded. At first the Pope refused, but during the night Christ appeared to him in a dream and told him to repair the Church, which had begun to fall down. Innocent received the man again and told him to go out with his companions and preach. The man was Francis of Assisi. This was the start of the Franciscan order, which is still a very important religious order today.

But personal interest and conflicts again divided the Church, beginning with the papal election in 1304. The conclave (the word comes from the Latin for a "key", and indicates that the process of election takes place behind locked doors) to find

A painting of
St. Francis of Assisi,
by the famous artist
Giotto

a successor went on for nine months until a Frenchman, who took the name of Clement V, was finally chosen. The Italian cardinals summoned Clement to Rome to be crowned, but instead he went to France and invited them to the ceremony there. There, at Lyons, in the presence of the French King, Philip IV (a fierce opponent of the power of the popes), Clement was crowned. During the ceremony, the papal crown was

29

The Palace of the Popes in Avignon, France

knocked off his head—many saw this as a sign of approaching trouble.

The trouble was not long in coming, for Clement did not return to Rome, but, under pressure from the French king, stayed in France, at Avignon. The dismay felt by the people of Rome was made all the worse when the Pope's own church, the Basilica of the Lateran, was burned to the ground in May, 1308.

When another Frenchman was elected to succeed Clement, the people of Rome decided to elect their own Pope, Nicholas V. He did not last long—he fled from Rome. It was not until 1377 that the rule of the popes in Avignon ended when Gregory XI returned to Rome. The fortunes of Christian Europe seemed to be at a very low ebb as, in addition to the troubles within the Church, millions of people throughout Europe had died from the Black Death.

Once again, however, Rome proved to be the "eternal city", and set about re-building, in all senses of the word.

And it was then that a development of particular significance to us took place. The former residence of the popes, the Lateran, had become a ruin and a pasture for sheep and goats. The Pope moved instead into another papal residence near the old Basilica of St. Peter and also near the *Castel Sant'Angelo*, the tomb of the Emperor Hadrian which had been made into a fortress and therefore offered some protection.

The Vatican had come into being.

Renaissance and Baroque Rome

At the beginning of the sixteenth century, developments took place which radically altered the way in which men viewed their own world. On October 12th, 1492, a sailor on Columbus's ship *Nina* sighted land: the New World of the Americas had been discovered. Approximately twenty years later, Copernicus, a student of science in Cracow (now in Poland), discovered that the earth went round the sun, and not vice-versa, as was thought until then.

The Renaissance was literally a "re-birth", especially in art and thought. The former glories of the Rome of the Emperors were brought back again in a programme of re-building that began with Nicholas V. The Vatican Library dates back to this time.

It was the reign of the Pope Sixtus IV and later that of his nephew Julius II which had the most lasting effect on Rome as a city, in terms of its art and architecture. The *Ponte Sisto*, (the Sistine Bridge) built for the Holy Year of 1475, bears the name of Sixtus, but much more famous is the chapel he built adjoining the Vatican Basilica: this is the Sistine Chapel, the personal chapel of the popes. The decoration of its ceiling and walls by Michelangelo makes it surely one of the most famous places in all Italy. (We will see more of the Sistine Chapel later in this book).

It was Julius II who decided to re-build St. Peter's Basilica, although he did not live to see it finished, for the work took more than a hundred years to complete.

Rome appeared to be thriving once more; but the Church was rocked almost to its foundations when, in 1517, a German monk called Martin Luther began a movement that came to be called the Reformation. This split the Christian Church once again.

At first pointing out many of the abuses which had crept in, Luther then went on to deny the authority of the Pope and to challenge many of the notions which lay at the very root of the traditional teaching of the Church.

The Church's "Counter-Reformation" led to the founding of the Society of Jesus (the "Jesuits" in 1540, the establishment of the Holy Office (fore-runner of today's Sacred Congregation for the Doctrine of the Faith, about which we will hear more later) and the Council of Trent, which met in the north of Italy in 1545. The Council's importance lies in its reaffirmation of certain doctrines of the Catholic faith which Luther and other people in the Reformation movement had denied. It also brought about some reforms within the Church, such as making provision for the proper and effective training of priests and clarifying the procedure for the appointment of bishops.

This was also the beginning of a style of architecture known as "Baroque", which seems to reflect the self-confidence of the Church after the attacks of the Reformers. The style is more ornate than what had gone before, more majestic and impres-

The Trevi Fountain, an example of the flamboyant and dramatic architecture of the Baroque period. Three coins thrown into the fountain over the left shoulder are said to ensure safe return to Rome

The Gesù, the principal church of the Jesuits. The tomb of their founder, St. Ignatius Loyola, is surmounted by this splendid altar

sive to the eye. Many of the churches of Rome are built in this style, such as the *Gesù*, the church of the Jesuits. Fountains like the boat in the Piazza di Spagna, the Fountain of the Four Rivers in the Piazza Navona and the famous Trevi Fountain all date from this period, and reflect a more dramatic approach to architecture and art. The embracing arms of the colonnade in front of St. Peter's were built at this time, too.

The Unification of Italy

It is easy to forget that Italy has been a united country for just over a hundred years. It was only in 1861 that the kingdom of Italy was formally proclaimed by a government meeting in Turin—the capital was not yet in Rome; for, although the Papal States had by now been lost to the new kingdom, Rome itself was still held by the Pope.

In 1864 the capital of the kingdom of Italy was transferred from Turin to Florence, but there still remained what was called "the Roman question"—the status of Rome and the pope within the new kingdom.

The Pope's position had been protected by Napoleon III, but this ended with the defeat of Napoleon in the war between France and Prussia in 1870. In the same year the troops of Victor Emmanuel, the first king of Italy, moved on Rome. The walls of the city were breached at the gate known as the Porta Pia, and the power of the popes as important political and territorial rulers came to an end.

A month after its fall, Rome was declared the capital of Italy. Pope Pius IX refused to deal with the new rulers of the city, and to accept the offer of settlement that was made, even though he was guaranteed complete freedom to exercise his authority as head of the Church, and allowed to keep the

36

The statue of Pope Pius IX, in front of St. Peter's Basilica

Vatican. He withdrew into the Vatican, and remained there as its prisoner until his death in 1878. It was not until 1929 that the situation was finally resolved by the agreement between Pope Pius XII and Mussolini. This agreement, known as the Lateran Treaty, formally established the Vatican City as a sovereign state; while the Holy See, in its turn, agreed to recognize Rome as the capital of Italy. The Roman Catholic Faith was pronounced the sole religion of the State, and the Vatican's independence in international affairs was guaranteed. A financial settlement was also reached in respect of the territories that had been lost by the ruler of the Papal States.

And so the position of the Vatican City State was made clear. The Pope was free to pursue a mission more in keeping with his position – a mission that is concerned with the spread of the message of Christ. His capacity to do this is greatly increased because as well as being the Bishop of Rome, he is the present successor of St. Peter and the one who enjoys the teaching authority of Christ. He is also a Head of State recognized as such in the community of the nations of the world. But it is important to recognize that distinction: the Vatican really has no purpose other than to exist for the Pope and for the Roman Catholic Church. If there were no Roman Catholic Church, there would be no reason for the Vatican to exist. The Pope very rarely acts simply as Head of State: his authority is truly exercised through the Holy See, and so often when we speak of "The Vatican" it is really the Holy See to which we are referring, for we want to talk about the work of the Roman Catholic Church, not a small area in Rome.

So the Vatican is what remains of what was once an enormous area in central Italy known as the Papal States. Now it is the place from which the Roman Catholic Church is administered, because it is the place in which the head of that Church, the Pope, has his residence.

As well as containing the papal residence within its walls, the Vatican also contains one of the most impressive collections

A long gallery in one of the Vatican Museums, with statues and carved friezes

of art in the world in its galleries and museums. It contains, too, many of the offices through which the Church, a community of seven hundred million people throughout the world, is run.

It is at those offices we shall look first, for they are at the centre of the institution which we know as the Catholic Church.

The Cardinals and the Sacred Congregations

The cardinals are the Pope's advisers, and for over 800 years they alone have been responsible for the election of the Pope – although since the time of Pope Paul VI (1971), those cardinals over the age of eighty no longer have the right to cast a vote in this election process.

The election takes place in a conclave, or assembly ("under lock and key") to ensure that there is no pressure from outside to influence decisions. The first election to be held in this way was in 1271 when the election had gone on for three years! Finally, the cardinals were locked in and told that they would not be released until they came out with a result. Needless to say, the election did not drag on for much longer.

When the Pope dies, in theory all the appointments made in the administrative offices of the Holy See cease to be, and the running of the Church becomes the responsibility of one of the cardinals, called the "Camerlengo", or Chamberlain. As well as making arrangements for the funeral of the dead Pope, he must also make arrangements for the election of his successor. It is he, then, who summons cardinals to Rome from all over the world into the conclave in the Sistine Chapel. This conclave must gather within twenty days of the Pope's death.

The voting takes place after the door has been locked and

sealed by the head of the Papal Household and the Commandant of the Swiss Guard. The cardinals each write their candidate's name on a slip of paper and then place this on the altar. If one candidate gains a majority of two-thirds plus one vote, then the election is over. The voting slips are put into an oven from which the smoke is visible to the people waiting below in the Square of St. Peter's. White smoke means that a new Pope has been found, and this news is officially announced by the chief cardinal from the balcony. Formerly, straw was put in with the voting slips, and the colour of the smoke was determined by whether the straw was dry or damp. Nowadays, chemicals are used instead.

The new Pope emerges, dressed already in the traditional white cassock, to the acclaim of the crowd, to give his first blessing. It is a moment of tremendous joy and excitement, as well as of great significance for the Church, for the unbroken line of succession from St. Peter is being carried on.

The cardinals' normal function, however, is within the offices through which the administration of the Catholic Church is done. The term that covers the whole of this administrative section within the Vatican is the "Curia", or more precisely "the Roman Curia", for each bishop has his Curia.

Although many of the cardinals live in their own countries and are responsible for a diocese, a number of them work permanently in Rome as heads of the various departments.

The man who is closest to the Pope is the Cardinal Secretary of State. The Secretariat of State, whose offices are within the

Letterheads of some of the offices of the Holy See, in English, Italian and Latin

Apostolic Palace, the Pope's own residence, is generally responsible for putting the Pope's decisions into practice. The Cardinal Secretary of State is assisted by an Archbishop called his "Substitute" and by a large number of priests and religious in the various sections that deal with different languages; for most of the enormous volume of correspondence that is addressed to the Pope comes through the Secretariat of State, and an effort is made to answer each letter that is written.

The Secretary of State is responsible for the Pope's dealings with Heads of State and his international affairs in general, and the Holy See's own diplomatic service is run from here. Each week the "diplomatic bag" leaves the Secretariat of State for each of the nunciatures or delegations throughout the

42

world (except for the smaller ones which might not have enough business to need this sort of weekly contact with the Holy See).

The Cardinal Secretary of State is also head of another department, called the Council for the Public Affairs of the Church. If we can regard the Cardinal Secretary of State as a sort of Prime Minister of the Pope, then we might regard the Council for the Public Affairs of the Church as a sort of Foreign Office. This office deals with civil and international matters and is therefore not totally independent but works in harmony with the Secretariat of State. Together, these two offices main-

The "diplomatic bag", a privilege conceded to all embassies, including those of the Holy See

tain a large degree of control over a third office, called the Pontifical Commission for Social Communications. We will come across this later in connection with Vatican Radio and the Vatican's newspaper.

But once again it must be clearly understood that the position of the Holy See in international affairs depends on the existence of the Catholic Church rather than on the territory of the Vatican City State. The existence of the Vatican ensures the Pope's independence and freedom in the field of international affairs, but when he speaks he does not speak as a Head of State but as the spiritual leader of the world's Catholics. A Roman Catholic in a small village in England and another on a farm in Australia have this one thing in common: their spiritual leader is the Pope, the Bishop of Rome. Each Roman Catholic belongs to a parish (or a religious community) and the head of that parish, the parish priest or pastor, is under the authority of the bishop of the diocese in which that parish is situated. That bishop, although independent to a certain extent to make decisions for his own diocese and for the priests and people under him, listens to the voice of the Holy Father in Rome and, before he is made a bishop, takes an oath of obedience and loyalty to the Pope. It is this particular relationship with the Pope and his teaching authority, derived from Jesus Christ through St. Peter and his successors, that guarantees the unity and the special nature of the Catholic Church.

The Church is administered and governed like any other large institution. The offices responsible for the most important aspects of this work are called "Sacred Congregations", and most important among these is the Sacred Congregation for the Doctrine of the Faith ("Doctrine" means "teaching").

The Sacred Congregations are like the ministries of national governments; and the Sacred Congregation for the Doctrine of the Faith was the first to be established (as the Holy Office) in 1542, to defend the Church against heresy (false teaching, contrary to the belief of the Church). Nowadays it is less concerned with fighting heresy and more concerned with the spread of the faith; and for this purpose it engages theologians who have made a special study of different aspects of the Catholic faith. This Sacred Congregation deals with all matters that concern faith or morals, such as the clarification of ideas that might not be acceptable as part of the faith of the Church. Its decisions are made after each question is submitted first to a body of consultors for their reflection and opinion and then passed on to a committee (the meaning of the word "Congregation") of cardinals. But it is not their decision which is final: the decision is ultimately the Pope's.

The idea of the local church is most important for an understanding of the Roman Catholic Church, for though the whole Church looks to Rome for teaching and leadership, the Church is divided into dioceses under the authority of a bishop. The choice of men to look after the different dioceses is most important, for they must be good leaders and men who are sound in their own faith if they are to help others in their faith and understanding.

The choice of bishops is the responsibility of the Sacred Congregation for Bishops.

When a diocese becomes vacant (through the death or retirement, usually at 75, of the former bishop), the process of finding a worthy successor begins. The Holy See's representative (the Apostolic Nuncio or Delegate) plays a most important part in this. He is appointed to act on behalf of the Holy See to make enquiries and submit to the Sacred Congregation for Bishops a detailed report and the names of the three most likely candidates. When the Sacred Congregation meets to discuss the report and the three candidates, their own report is submitted to the Holy Father for the final decision.

There are nine Sacred Congregations in all, covering the principal aspects of the Church's activity. One, the Sacred Congregation for Eastern Churches, is responsible for those Catholics in the East who are part of the Church of Rome and give obedience to the Pope but have a different tradition in many things, especially in their liturgy (their worship in church).

The practice of the liturgy is the responsibility of the Sacred Congregation for Sacraments and Divine Worship. Most of the work that has occupied this particular department over the last twenty years has been a result of a major change that took place after a meeting of bishops from all over the world in 1963. This meeting, the Second Vatican Council, called by Pope John XXIII, introduced changes in many areas in the Church; and one of the most widely felt was the decision to abandon the

46

The view from the top of the dome of St. Peter's over the Apostolic Palace, the Sistine Chapel and the Vatican Museums

use of Latin alone as the language in which the liturgy was celebrated. Until 1964, mass was said throughout the world in Latin, as it had been for sixteen hundred years, but the Vatican Council decided that the people would benefit far more from their worship in church if it were done in their own language. And so, in the years since that decision was first put into effect, the Sacred Congregation for Sacraments and Divine Worship has been producing and approving translations and new versions of the words used at mass and in all of the seven sacraments of the Church—baptism, confirmation,

47

the eucharist, penance or reconciliation, holy orders (by which a priest is ordained), marriage and the anointing of the sick. In all cases it is not simply the language which has changed: different aspects have been emphasized as the Church's own understanding has developed and changed.

The Sacred Congregation for the Clergy exists to help priests in their work. The number of priests in the Church has dropped in recent years, and the Sacred Congregation must ensure that priests are all the more effective in their ministry. A similar organization exists for those who take religious vows (those we refer to most commonly as "monks" and "nuns") and live in community, but often work outside their community among the people. This organization, the Sacred Congregation for Religious and Lay Institutes, also looks after groups of people who do not join religious communities but who form groups to pray and work together.

The Church has always been missionary, which means that it has always been trying to spread the message of the Gospel to places where it was not known. The Roman Catholic Faith was taken to the South American continent by the Spaniards, and today missionaries still go to South America to preach and work for the social welfare of its peoples. Missionaries also work in Africa, and in other parts of what we call "The Third World" which do not have enough priests and religious of their own. These missionaries are looked after by the Sacred Congregation for the Propagation of the Faith (more commonly referred to as "Propaganda Fide"). There are also

48

countries in Europe, however, which are its concern, for they are no longer able to practise their faith openly.

The Sacred Congregation for Catholic Education is responsible for all levels of Catholic education, but above all for the training of young men for the priesthood.

The Sacred Congregation for the Causes of Saints examines the lives of those who are held up as examples of Christian virtue and who might be regarded as worthy of being called "Saint".

The Offices of the Roman Catholic Church

In addition to the Sacred Congregations, there are many other offices which play an important part in the running of the Church.

The Holy See has its own courts but, as one would expect, their work is concerned with matters of the Church rather than with infringements of laws within the Vatican itself. The highest of the three courts of the Holy See is the Supreme Tribunal of the Apostolic Signatura and, like the second, the Sacred Roman Rota, it is a court of appeal. Much of the work of these two is concerned with marriage cases. There is no divorce in the Catholic Church, but in some instances the Church judges (through its courts in the local diocese or, on appeal, in Rome) that, for some reason, it is right to say that the marriage never really took place, even though the outward ceremony was performed. If, for instance, a person went through the ceremony of marriage but did not really want to get married, then the Church would say that there was not a proper marriage. Or if one of the partners was deceiving the other, so that he or she was marrying in ignorance of the truth about the other partner, then again the Church would consider that a true marriage had not taken place.

The third court is the Sacred Apostolic Penitentiary, which

Church dignitaries being presented to Pope John Paul II on his visit to Great Britain in 1982

deals with other offences against the faith of the Catholic Church.

Since the Second Vatican Council, the Roman Catholic Church has had much greater contact than previously with other Churches and other faiths. The Secretariat for Christian Unity deals with unity among Christians, although relations with the Jewish faith also come within its sphere of concern; and the Secretariat for non-Christians deals with relations between the Roman Catholic Church and beliefs such as

The courtyard of the Cancelleria Palace, now the offices of the Courts of the Holy See, but originally built for the nephew of Pope Sixtus IV, who paid for its construction with what he won in one night, gambling!

Buddhism and Islam. The Secretariat for non-believers attempts to meet the challenge of atheism in the world today— atheists say that there is no God at all.

Other commisions, committees and councils deal with the laity (the name given to those who are not priests or religious— they are the "ordinary" believers), the family, justice and peace – there is even a special commission to look after migrants and tourists. And with such a rich artistic tradition, it is inevit-

52

able that the Holy See should have a commission for art and for archaeology, as well as another for science.

An organization as vast as the Roman Catholic Church must be involved in financial administration – the Holy See has to finance its diplomatic service, cover the great costs of running the many offices within the Curia, and see to the transfer of funds to the poorer missions in the Third World. It is not realistic to pretend that the Church does not need money and that it should not be involved in investment. Catholics throughout the world do contribute generously to a fund known as "Peter's Pence", but this would be inadequate to meet all the financial needs of the Holy See. The Holy See also owns property, and all this is the responsibility of the office of the Administration of the Patrimony of the Holy See – this is the correct title for what is usually simply called "The Vatican Bank".

Like any organization round a Head of State, the Papal Household requires thorough and efficient administration. The Prefecture of the Papal Household deals with papal ceremonies, papal audiences and all the other official activity around the person of the Pope himself. With the Secretariat of State, the Prefecture of the Papal Household must see to the arrangements for the Pope's travels abroad—this has become a regular occurrence in past years, a far cry from the days when the Pope was "the prisoner of the Vatican".

Anyone wishing to enter the Vatican must pass through one of a few gates. One of these is to the left of the Basilica of

St. Peter's, under the arch known as "The Arch of the Bells". There is another gate in the wall that leads off to the right of the colonnade: this is the *Porta Sant'Anna*, for it is just beside what is, in fact, the parish church of the Vatican—the little Church of Saint Anne.

At either of these gates the visitor will be stopped (unless he is recognized as a cardinal or an archbishop—in that case he will receive a smart salute in greeting). The guards on these gates are the famous Swiss Guards, dressed in their distinctive and colourful uniform which is said to have been

A Vatican gateway. All visitors to the Vatican have to pass through one of the gateways guarded by the Swiss Guard

designed by Michelangelo. And they are truly Swiss! In 1506 a corps of troops from Switzerland arrived before the Papal Palace and were received by Pope Julius II. They were appointed to guard the person of the Pope himself and the Apostolic Palace. And this is still their function: the hundred soldiers live in their barracks just inside the *Porta Sant'Anna*. They are all Catholic and, by a special arrangement with Switzerland, can serve in the Swiss Guard of the Pope when they have done their military service at home.

This vast complex of offices and people is all part of what the Holy See understands as its mission in the world: to spread good-will, peace and belief in Christ. We have looked already at some of the ways in which that work is done or assisted. There are two other ways in which the mission of the Catholic Church is carried out or supported which deserve attention.

The Holy See's Diplomatic Relations

The position of the Pope is unique in many ways. His position within the international community is unique because, although he is principally concerned with the spiritual welfare of the seven hundred million Roman Catholics throughout the world, he is also a Head of State. And as Head of State he is entitled to send and receive ambassadors. The Holy See maintains a world-wide diplomatic service.

An ambassador is someone who is appointed to act on behalf of and in the name of whoever sends him. The Bishop of Rome has been sending representatives to act on his authority for a long time—in the year 343 the Emperor Constantine summoned a council or meeting at Sardica, to which the Bishop of Rome sent a delegation.

This sort of thing, however, was not like the sending of ambassadors today. These delegates were sent for a particular occasion, and it was not until the sixteenth century that the Holy See began to send representatives of papal authority to other countries on a more permanent and stable basis.

Today the Holy See sends representatives to nearly a hundred and twenty states (as well as to the United Nations and to the European Economic Community in Brussels), although in many instances one man will act as representative to a number of countries—the Holy See's ambassador in Scandinavia, for example, is responsible for Denmark, Norway, Sweden, Finland and Iceland.

These ambassadors of the Holy See are not given the title "ambassador", but are given titles which are used only of the Pope's representatives. In many countries (usually those which are considered Roman Catholic) the papal represent- ative is appointed as Dean or head of the Diplomatic Corps in that country: in that situation he is called a "Nuncio". Where the Holy See's ambassador is not the Dean of the Diplomatic Corps he is called a "Pro-Nuncio". In some countries, too, he is not fully accredited as an ambassador (meaning that there are not full diplomatic relations between that country and the Holy See) and there he is given the title of "Apostolic Delegate".

Recently the United States of America, Scandinavia (as a group) and Britain have established full diplomatic relations which they did not have before—three of the Scandinavian countries had full relations, two did not. Britain had had a representative at the Holy See since 1914, but it was not until 1938 that an Apostolic Delegate was appointed to London. In March, 1982, Archbishop Bruno B. Heim presented his Letters of Credence to Her Majesty the Queen, and thus became the first Apostolic Pro-Nuncio to occupy the house on Wimbledon Common where the Pope was received as a guest on his recent visit to Britain in the same year. The decree formally establishing diplomatic relations between the Holy

IOANNES PAVLVS PP. II

Ad perpetuam rei memoriam

Quo amplius mutuae amicitiae atque necessitudinis rationes inter hanc Apostolicam Sedem et Magnam Britanniam iam feliciter initae proveherentur, Nobis peropportunum est visum Nuntiaturam Apostolicam in ea Natione condere. Hanc igitur ob causam re bene considerata diligenterque perpensa deque plenitudine Nostrae potestatis, harum Litterarum vi, Apostolicam Nuntiaturam in Magna Britannia constituimus, eidemque omnia et singula officia, privilegia atque indulta deferimus quae huiusmodi Legationum propria sunt. Decernimus praeterea ut conditae Nuntiaturae Apostolicae Sedes Londinii in clarissima urbe Regni principe ponatur. Quae denique per praesentes Litteras statuimus vim suam habere nunc et in posterum volumus, contrariis nihil obstantibus. Datum Romae, apud Sanctum Petrum, sub anulo Piscatoris, die XVII mensis Januarii, anno MCMLXXXII, Pontificatus Nostri quarto.

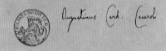

Augustinus Card. Casaroli

The decree formally establishing diplomatic relations between the Holy See and the Court of St. James's in the United Kingdom

See and Great Britain is shown in the photograph. It is in Latin and is signed by the Pope's Secretary of State. The seal depicts St. Peter in his fishing boat and the text says that the decree is given *sub anulo Piscatoris*, "under the ring (seal) of the Fisherman".

The Pope's ambassadors do not represent the Vatican City State. They represent the authority of the Holy See, which is not connected with territory or many of the other matters that are the concern of other ambassadors and diplomats. The Holy See does not trade and so it does not need to appoint a diplomat with commercial interests. The Swiss Guard cannot really be considered any longer as an army—this would be a contradiction of the Holy See's mission and aims in the world—

and so there are no military attachés in Papal Nunciatures.

The Holy See sends its representatives, then, not to safeguard its own national interests, for it has none. Its representatives are there above all to guarantee close links between the Holy See and the Church of each particular country, but without attempting to control that Church by limiting the authority of its own bishops. The highest teaching authority of the Church is the Bishop of Rome, and his representatives are one means of spreading that teaching throughout the Roman Catholic community over the world, and then to all those who share the Holy See's concern and work for peace and justice in the world.

Some of the crowd waiting excitedly for a glimpse of the Pope

Vatican Radio and "L'Osservatore Romano"

Vatican Radio is part of a much larger organization within the Holy See which is concerned with the spread of the Church's teaching through the "media", including the press and television.

The Pontifical Commission for Social Communications was begun in 1948 as an experimental commission to look into the possibilities that the cinema offered as a teaching tool. In 1954 its responsibility was extended to cover radio and television; and then, under Pope Paul VI in 1964, it received the name which it bears today and became linked directly with the Office of the Secretariat of State. It is this commission which runs the Vatican's press office, established in 1968.

Vatican Radio is situated within the Vatican itself, in and near the old Vatican Observatory. Its monthly programme bulletin is sent to 157 countries and its programmes can be heard world-wide in languages as diverse as Romanian, Arabic and Esperanto. The programme content is again part of the mission of the Church: stereo broadcasts of music and news bulletins are repeated in the principal languages, but most of the short programmes are distinctly religious, as one would expect. Mass celebrated in the Vatican is broadcast in Latin every day and the rosary is said in the evening.

For many Catholics this presence is the only contact they might have with their faith. Vatican Radio is a way of reaching into areas where there is no religious freedom and where the practice of religion is difficult or impossible. For this reason there tend to be more broadcasts directed towards communist countries, for instance, than towards the rest of Europe. It is said that authorities who might be opposed to the spread of religious ideas deliberately attempt to block or disturb the Vatican's transmissions by broadcasting on or around the same frequency.

Vatican Radio is run by a Jesuit, with a staff of some thirty Jesuits working full-time with him—although, naturally, the actual content of its transmissions depends on the Holy See itself. Apart from the central staff, over two hundred others are employed by Vatican Radio for its foreign-language services.

Over the years, of course, as its importance has grown and techniques have developed, so the service has expanded. Apart from the central office within the Vatican, there are offices in the new buildings at the top of the Via della Conciliazione, approaching St. Peter's; and the actual transmitting is done from a station about sixteen kilometres (ten miles) outside Rome.

The *Osservatore Romano* (literally "The Roman Observer") is not, in fact, the official newspaper of the Holy See: there is none. The official publication of the Holy See is a document called the *Acta Apostolicae Sedis* ("The Acts of the Holy See")

61

L'Osservatore Romano and the Acta Apostolicae Sedis, two of the regular publications of the Vatican's printing press

which includes all official documents and statements. The *Osservatore Romano* instead calls itself "a daily political and religious newspaper" on its cover, although it does give its origin as the Vatican City and is, to all intents and purposes, an official mouthpiece of the Holy See, which controls and finances it.

The paper was founded in 1861 and its daily publication in Italian is summarized in weekly editions in English, French, Spanish, Portuguese, German and Polish.

It does report, as its title claims, events from the world of politics; but, like the Vatican Radio, its function is to be seen as part of the mission of the Pope and the Roman Catholic Church to proclaim the message of Christ.

St. Peter's Basilica

The Vatican territory is very small, covering only 0.44 square kilometres (0.17 square miles). Within this small area, however, is a great artistic heritage. In 1960 the United Nations included the whole of the Vatican in its "International Register of Cultural Works under Special Protection". Pride of place must surely go to St. Peter's Basilica, the dome of which rises to a height of 132 metres (433 feet) and dominates the Vatican skyline.

As can be seen here, there are no "high-rise" blocks in central Rome. The skyline is dominated by the dome of St. Peter's.

The Via della
Conciliazione, the broad
thoroughfare cleared by
Mussolini to present a
fitting approach to
St. Peter's Basilica

We have already considered why this particular spot is so important, and have seen that it is principally for its connection with St. Peter that so many people come to the Basilica. It is a place of pilgrimage.

Approaching the Basilica along the Via della Conciliazione (built by Mussolini to symbolize the agreement between the Vatican and Italy reached in the Lateran Treaty of 1929), the dome can be seen in its full glory. As one crosses the Piazza in front of the Basilica, the dome vanishes behind the facade that stretches across the front of St. Peter's. This facade and the colonnade that seems to embrace the Piazza were the last additions to the building. In the centre of the facade is the *loggia* or balcony from which the Pope gives his first blessing *Urbi et Orbi*, "to the City and to the World".

The door on the right leading into the Basilica is usually sealed, for this is the "Holy Door", opened only once every twenty-five years during the Holy Year (in 1983 Pope John Paul proclaimed a special Holy Year as a Jubilee of the Redemption, for it is held that Christ died and rose in A.D. 33). Then the Pope himself knocks at this door with a silver hammer and the door is opened to admit pilgrims to the tomb of the Apostle.

Once inside, the sheer size of the building gradually dawns on the visitor. There are marks on the floor comparing the length of this church with other great churches. As we walk

Looking up the nave of St. Peter's towards the High Altar

The interior of the dome of St. Peter's above the tomb of the Apostle. The ornate pillar is part of the canopy erected above the altar by Bernini

towards the altar, the first name we come to is that of St. Paul's in London: this measures 158 metres (518 feet), against the 186 metres (610 feet) of St. Peter's Basilica. The ceiling is 44 metres (144 feet) above our heads.

Apart from the altar above the tomb of St. Peter, there are two particular attractions for the visitor. The first of these is immediately to our right as we come in. It is a carving of the dead Christ, supported across the lap of his mother, Mary. The statue is Michelangelo's famous *Pietà* (the name given to other representations, too, of this same moment). It is the only work that Michelangelo signed, and his signature is carved into the band that crosses the madonna's breast. The work is all the more remarkable when one considers that Michelangelo was only 24 years old when he did it.

The other feature is a statue of St. Peter. At first it was thought to be a work from the fifth century, but later it was discovered to come from the thirteenth. Its most striking feature is that the right foot, which juts forward, has been worn smooth. This has been done over the centuries by the faithful who come to the tomb of the Apostle and who kiss or just touch this statue of St. Peter as a gesture of their faith in the Church that was founded on "The Rock" (the meaning of the Greek name which Jesus gave to Peter).

At the far end of the Basilica is a beautiful window depicting

Bernini's window above the "cathedra" of St. Peter. The dove is the symbol of the Holy Spirit

A major attraction for visitors to the Vatican is Michelangelo's Pietà, a statue of the dead Christ, supported across the lap of his mother Mary

the Holy Spirit in the form of a dove. This is just above an ornate piece of carving which covers what is said to be the chair or throne actually used by St. Peter himself. This is particularly significant, for the Latin word for "throne" is *cathedra*. This gives us the English word "cathedral", meaning the place where a bishop has his chair or throne. And we use chair in the same sense when we speak of a professor at a university who holds the chair in some branch of teaching. For this is just what the chair is—the symbol of St. Peter's (and his successors') authority to teach. This is what we mean by "The Holy See".

68

It is the See or Seat of Peter, the authority given to him by Christ to instruct and teach the Christian faith.

There is another smaller chapel not far from St. Peter's, but there is no access to it here. To enter it we must go round the walls of the Vatican and in through the museums. It is a chapel that is justly famous for a number of reasons, and is named after the Pope who had it built. He was called Sixtus IV.

The Sistine Chapel

The Sistine Chapel ("Sistine" means "of Sixtus") is a rather simple and modest building. It is famous, however, the world over, principally for the way in which Pope Julius II had it decorated.

Julius II had seen Michelangelo's *Pietà* and had given him the job of building him a magnificent tomb. This project did not get far—only one of the statues planned was actually finished. This was the "Moses", now in the Church of St. Peter in Chains. There is a mark on the knee of the statue, said to be the result of an outburst by Michelangelo when he threw his hammer at the marble, demanding that the statue should speak to him. The statue's expression and stance are so expressive and life-like.

Work on the plans for the tomb was interrupted by another grandiose scheme of Pope Julius. The Pope had started the rebuilding of the Basilica of St. Peter's and, while the architect Bramante occupied himself with that work, Julius set Michelangelo to work on the ceiling of the Sistine Chapel. It is said that Bramante was jealous of Michelangelo and wanted to make sure that Michelangelo did not get his job; he therefore suggested to Julius that Michelangelo might paint the ceiling. He knew that Michelangelo was not really a painter but was a sculptor and architect; if Michelangelo failed to please the Pope with his painting, then Bramante's own job was safe.

Although he was asked at first only to paint the twelve Apostles into the *lunettes* (the spaces where the arches above the windows meet the ceiling), Michelangelo decided to paint the whole ceiling.

The result was astounding. Michelangelo worked alone, painting directly onto wet plaster (a technique that we call "fresco", and a technique that he had not used before). He had to paint upside-down, and it is said that for months afterwards he could not read a letter unless it was held above him and he tilted his head back.

The other great masterpiece in the Chapel is also Michelangelo's. It is the painting of the Last Judgement that covers the wall above the altar. It was painted much later than the ceiling (twenty years later). Michelangelo was given the task by Clement VII in 1533, but just after he arrived in Rome the following year, Clement died. If Michelangelo thought that this was the end of the idea, he was wrong. The new Pope, Paul III, was just as keen on the idea and work started

Part of the ceiling of the Sistine Chapel, painted by Michelangelo—
one of the most famous art treasures in the Vatican

in January, 1536. It was October, 1541, before the work was finally unveiled. The effect on the Pope was dramatic. He is said to have fallen on his knees and begged God for a merciful judgement for himself.

Michelangelo was sixty years old at this time.

The Sistine Chapel is one of the truly great masterpieces of art in Europe, although not all have appreciated its artistic value. Michelangelo painted all the figures naked, and Pius IV

A detail from Michelangelo's painting of the Last Judgement

ordered a man named Daniele di Volterra to paint some clothing on them—for this, he gained a place in history and was nicknamed "the breeches-maker". At least the painting escaped more lightly than it would have done under Clement VIII if he had done what he first intended: the work so shocked him that he wanted the wall whitewashed completely!

The Sistine Chapel is also renowned for what happens in there. It is the Pope's own Chapel and, as we saw earlier, it is there that the Pope first knows that he has been chosen by the men who were, until that moment, his fellow cardinals. When the required majority is reached, the new Pope leaves the Sistine Chapel dressed in the red-trimmed black cassock of a cardinal. When he returns a few moments later he has replaced his black cassock with white.

Throughout history, the Church has been a great sponsor of art, and even a brief look at painting through the ages will reveal how much of it is religious in character—the Sistine Chapel is one example of a work of art that resulted from the initiative of a Pope.

Much of what is contained in the Vatican's Museums does owe its origin to the Church, but there is much else that is pagan in origin and has been gathered by successive popes who were patrons of the arts. In fact, the beginning of the collection can be traced back to the same Pope Julius II who commissioned the painting of the Sistine ceiling.

The museums are the only part of the Vatican which the

visitor sees. From the top of the dome of St. Peter's there is a view down into the Vatican Gardens; but they are calm, well ordered and peaceful, for visitors here are rare. The gardens occupy the north-west part of the Vatican, within the walls built around the Vatican between 1550 and 1640 for its defence.

The eastern side of the Vatican is occupied by the Vatican Palace itself. This is not just one building, but a collection of buildings that house the papal appartments and other offices intimately connected with the running of the Church (it is here that the Secretariat of State is found). Here, too, are the Vatican Secret Archives and the Library, which house some of the oldest treasures of the Holy See; for the Treasury itself was repeatedly pillaged by the invaders who came to Rome to destroy and rob.

A view from the top of the dome of St. Peter's into the Vatican Gardens, looking down onto the Palace of the Government of the Vatican City

People gathered in St. Peter's Square for the Pope's Sunday Blessing

The Pope lives on the top floor of the palace, and on Sundays at noon he traditionally comes to his window to pray with the crowds who assemble in the square below and to give them his blessing. On the floor below the papal apartments are the rooms where he holds private audiences with the cardinals from the Sacred Congregations and with other clerics.

For the general audiences, however, thousands gather on a Wednesday either in the square below or in the hall that was

A view of the Vatican from the Castel Sant'Angelo. On the right is the path along the wall joining the Castel Sant'Angelo to the Vatican

built for this purpose behind the colonnade on the other side of the square from the Apostolic Palace. Designed by the Italian architect Pier Luigi Nervi, the Audience Hall can hold 12,000 people standing. It is slightly sunken and does not seem out of place among such old and famous buildings as the Basilica which towers above it, even though it was completed only in 1971. It is used when the weather will not permit the Pope to hold his audience in the open. It was during one of these open-air audiences, as he was being driven through the crowd so that as many people as possible would have a glimpse of him from close-up, that Pope John Paul II was shot in May, 1982.

Even within the Vatican, security has now, tragically, become a problem.

This is a reminder that many of the problems and requirements of the running of any other country also face the Vatican. Hence the existence of the office of the *Governatorato*, from which the Vatican (as distinct from the Holy See) is administered. This will allow us to see what interesting aspects of the Vatican are not directly associated with the religious mission of the Holy See.

The Vatican City State

The Vatican Railway was built in the 1930s, continuing a line that runs north of Rome. Now it carries little, and is used only for the import of goods into the Vatican. The Vatican itself, of course, is not a producer, and has no exports (except perhaps for the work done in the mosaic factory in the Vatican Gardens). The Pope today is either driven in one of the white "Popemobiles" (the specially converted Range Rover which he used when he visited Great Britain in 1982 was later presented to the Holy See), or in a black limousine bearing the number plate SCV 1. (SCV stands for *Stato della Città del Vaticano*, the Vatican City State). He saves time, too, by flying. The Italian

Stamps from the papacies of John Paul I and John Paul II, both elected in 1978, the "Year of the Three Popes"

The flag of the Vatican City State, with the papal coat of arms

Air Force gave him the use of a helicopter, and this is used mostly for trips within Italy, especially between the Vatican and the papal villa outside Rome at Castelgandolfo.

Because there is not really an economy within the Vatican, there are no taxes. The Vatican does mint its own coins (the same size and denomination as Italian currency) but it does not print notes. Like its stamps, the coins are collectors' items rather than a vital part of an economic system. Its stamps are real enough, for there is a Post Office in the Vatican and its stamps are not inter-changeable with those of Italy: Vatican stamps are to be posted within the Vatican and not in Italy,

79

A coin from the papacy of Paul VI, bearing his arms

and vice-versa. Letters posted in the Vatican are then sent to Switzerland, strangely enough, before being sorted and distributed. These things, the coinage and the postal system, do emphasize the fact that the Vatican is internationally recognized as an independent, self-governing state. It has its own flag, too, the yellow and white indicating the gold and silver of the two keys that are on the papal coat of arms. The two keys are the ones referred to in the passage in the Gospel when Christ hands over to St. Peter authority to govern his Church on earth—"I will give you the keys of the Kingdom of Heaven, and whatever you bind on earth shall be bound in heaven, and whatever you loose on earth shall be loosed in heaven".

The two keys, crossed and joined by a red cord, symbolize not only this power over earthly matters, but a power that is recognized also in heaven. Each Pope has his own coat of arms—a family shield, with the keys underneath it; but the arms of the Holy See are the keys surmounted by the papal "tiara", a ceremonial head-dress with three golden crowns on it. Since ceremonies and papal functions were made more simple by Pope John XXIII and his successors, the papal tiara has not been worn. The Holy See's coat of arms can be seen in the middle of the flag, either simply against the yellow and white background or, more clearly as here, on a red shield.

As a state, too, the Vatican issues passports. There are just over seven hundred inhabitants of the Vatican, although only just over half of those actually have citizenship, and many of these are in the Holy See's diplomatic service and so work abroad. No one is born within the Vatican, and so citizenship is conferred on those who work most closely within the Holy See or, like the Swiss Guard, within the Vatican's walls.

Until 1975 there was a bakery in the Vatican! There is still a petrol station from which the Vatican's employees can buy petrol much more cheaply than they can in Italy (because there is no tax), and food and other goods can also be bought quite cheaply from the one store. (It is said that things even themselves out because the Vatican's employees are not well paid!) Just inside the *Porta Sant' Anna* there is the Vatican Post Office, a pharmacy run by the *Fatebenefratelli*, the Brothers of St. John of God who run hospitals throughout the world (one is on the island in the middle of the River Tiber) and the Vatican's printing press where the newspaper and other publications are produced.

Here, too, is the public section of the Vatican's Bank and the Health Centre for its dependents. Alongside the workshops which look after the material of its buildings and their contents, there is a generating station for the electricity supply of this tiny state.

The Vatican's Extra-territorial Possessions

The territory of the Vatican does, however, extend beyond its walls. When the Lateran Treaty was drawn up between the Italian State and the Holy See in 1929, it was agreed that certain "territories", most of them within Rome, should remain the property of the Holy See. The most important of these is the Basilica of St. John Lateran and the Lateran Palace.

It is often wrongly assumed that St. Peter's Basilica is the Pope's own cathedral, and therefore the most important church in the Christian (Latin) community.

Because the first of these ideas is incorrect, however, so is the second. The Pope's cathedral is not St. Peter's; and the "mother church" of all churches is the Basilica of St. John Lateran, alongside the palace of the same name.

The name came from the Laterani, the family who originally owned the land until it was confiscated and given to the Church by the Roman Emperor Constantine. It was believed that he was baptized in the famous Baptistry adjoining the

82

The facade of the Basilica of St. John Lateran

Basilica, but this seems not to be the case. Like many, he delayed his baptism until he thought that he was towards the end of his life, in this way he reckoned that he stood a better chance of getting into Heaven!

The present Basilica preserves the shape of the original church, but through the centuries the Basilica of John Lateran was sacked by the Vandals, damaged in an earthquake and twice burned down.

Inside the church, above the main altar, there is a shrine which contains an old wooden table, supposedly the altar which St. Peter himself used.

The Lateran Palace now houses the offices of the diocese of Rome, but was originally built as a summer residence for the popes in 1386. It is hard to imagine now that this area was, until fairly recently, part of the Roman *campagna* or countryside. At the beginning of this century the English College in Rome owned its own vineyards just beside the Basilica. Now it is close to a suburb of wide, dusty streets lined with rather drab apartment blocks.

Joined to the Basilica of St. John Lateran by the Via Merulana is another of the four great basilicas, that of St. Mary Major, the first Church in Rome to be dedicated to the Mother of God. It was built in memory of the Council of Ephesus in the fifth century, for it was at this Council that the Motherhood of the Blessed Virgin was defined. There is a legend that the site of the Basilica was shown to the Pope through a miraculous fall of snow on the night of August 5th, but it seems that this legend was originally attached to another church on the Esquiline Hill.

More than any other of the basilicas, St. Mary Major seems to have preserved its ancient form inside, although it is richer in appearance now than it would have been at the beginning—the ceiling is decorated with what is said to be the first gold brought by the Spaniards from South America.

The fourth of the great basilicas is a little way outside the city walls, because it was there, on the Via Ostiense (the road leading to the old port of Ostia at the mouth of the Tiber) that St. Paul met his death. Another foundation of Constantine, this basilica stood largely unaltered until, tragically, it was destroyed by fire in 1823. It is said that Pope Pius VII, who was close to death at the time, had been disturbed by strange dreams the night before, but he was spared the sad news of the destruction of the basilica and died without knowing that it had burned to the ground. In the church there is a series of mosaic portraits of the popes from the time of St. Peter (many of them imaginative rather than actual portraits from life, obviously), and just before the fire, it was noticed that there was not enough room for another portrait. The people wondered what was going to happen, and many would say that the destruction of St. Paul's Outside the Walls (as it is properly called) was no surprise.

There are a number of other sites both in and around Rome which, by the terms of the concordat between Italy and the Holy See, are the property of the Vatican. The most famous, perhaps, in the Christian tradition, are the burial places known as the catacombs.

The name "catacomb" is correctly applied only to this type of burial place near Rome, even though they are found elsewhere. These burial places were described according to features by which they could be recognized. One was described as "the cemetery in the shady hollow" (in Greek *kata kumbas*), and it was this one which has given its name to them all.

Legend tells us that the early Christians used to flee to the catacombs during times of persecution to hide and to celebrate their masses, but there is no truth in this. First of all, they were not really very good places to hide, since everyone knew where they were! And secondly they would say mass not there (except perhaps at the time of an actual burial) but in private houses, before the change in the law under Constantine allowed them to build their own churches.

Roman law did not allow the burial or cremation of a body inside the city walls, and this is why the catacombs are located outside the ancient city boundaries. Also, the type of ground around Rome favours this type of cemetery: it is volcanic "tufa", a deposit from the long extinct volcanoes of the Alban Hills which is soft enough to dig into and which then hardens on contact with the air.

At first the Christians buried their dead in the common

The catacombs, showing clearly the niches in which the bodies were laid

burial places, and only later, around the beginning of the third century, did they begin to buy their own sites for exclusively Christian burial places. Some still bear the name of the person who either bought the land or gave it to the Christian community—Domitilla, Priscilla, Calistus.

More than forty such cemeteries have been discovered within a short distance of the walls that the Emperor Marcus Aurelius built around Rome. Sadly, many of them were looted through the centuries, as much by Christians as by pagan invaders. Local people used the marble for their buildings; and many of the inscriptions and bodies were taken to Christian churches, especially when it was thought that the body was that of a martyr who had died for the faith during one of the persecutions.

The Significance of the Vatican

It is convenient to end at this point, back where we began, for the time of the persecution takes us back to St. Peter and his own death at the hands of the Roman authorities.

St. Peter's death and burial place are commemorated in stone at the place where he was buried, in the cemetery on the Vatican Hill.

But it is not true to say that he is commemorated only in

Pope John Paul II and church dignitaries at the mass celebrated in Westminster Cathedral, London, during the Pope's visit in 1982

stone and in the things we can see. He lives still in the figure who appears on the balcony of the mighty Basilica above the bones of the fisherman from Galilee. For it is with the authority first given by Christ to Peter that the present pope, whoever he may be as you read this, teaches and preaches.

This is the significance of the Vatican, the place where the Holy See works to serve the needs of the world's 740 million Roman Catholics. Although most of them remain largely unaware of the Vatican and the 3,000 people working in its offices and various departments, they are all aware, to some extent at least, of the head of this vast and expanding institution. He is their spiritual leader, and he is also the Head of State of the Vatican.

The Successors of St. Peter

The title "pope", meaning "father", was originally used of any bishop. It was Gregory VII, in 1073, who said that it should be used only of the Bishop of Rome.

The shortest reign of a Pope was that of Stephen II, who died in the year 752 before he was actually crowned. His reign lasted just three days. The longest reign was that of Pope Pius IX, in the last century. He reigned for thirty-one years.

Benedict IX seems to have been the youngest Pope—he was elected in the year 1032 at the age of fifteen! In contrast, Pope Celestine II was eighty-five when he began his reign.

This century has seen the "Year of the Three Popes" when, in September 1978, John Paul I succeeded Paul VI. The reign of John Paul I, however, lasted just thirty-three days, and he was succeeded by John Paul II.

Most of the 263 Popes to date have been Italian, but the throne of St. Peter has also been occupied by a number of other nationalities. These include Popes from Greece, Syria, Dalmatia and Thracia (before the split between the Christian Church of the west and the Christian Church of the east in 1054), Germany, France and Spain. The only English Pope was Nicholas Breakspear, who chose the name Adrian IV on his election. He was probably born in St. Albans, in about the year 1100. There has also been one Portuguese Pope (John XXI, elected in 1276) and one Dutch Pope (Adrian VI, born in Utrecht, Holland, in 1459). Adrian VI was one of the few Popes to keep his own name when elected. The present Pope, John Paul II, is the first Polish Pope. In fact, he is the first non-Italian Pope for over four hundred years, since Adrian VI (1522-23).

St. Peter established his See at Antioch and then transferred it, in the year 42, to Rome, where he suffered martyrdom on 29 June 67. This is a list of his successors—the dates alongside each name are the dates of accession of the Popes.

St. Linus	AD 67	St. Melchiades	311
St. Anacletus or Cletus	76	St. Silvester I	314
St. Clement	88	St. Mark	336
St. Evaristus	97	St. Julius I	337
St. Alexander I	105	Liberius	352
St. Sixtus I	115	St. Damasus	366
St. Telesphorus	125	St. Siricius	384
St. Hyginus	136	St. Anastasius I	399
St. Pius I	140	St. Innocent I	401
St. Anicetus	155	St. Zozimus	417
St. Soter	166	St. Boniface I	418
St. Eleutherius	175	St. Celestine I	422
St. Victor I	189	St. Sixtus III	432
St. Zephyrinus	199	St. Leo the Great	440
St. Callistus I	217	St. Hilary	461
St. Urban I	222	St. Simplicius	468
St. Pontian	230	St. Felix III [II]	483
St. Anterus	235	St. Gelasius I	492
St. Fabian	236	Anastasius II	496
St. Cornelius	251	St. Symmachus	498
St. Lucius I	253	St. Hormisdas	514
St. Stephen I	254	St. John I	523
St. Sixtus II	257	St. Felix IV [III]	526
St. Dionysius	259	Boniface II	530
St. Felix I	269	John II	533
St. Eutychian	275	St. Agapitus	535
St. Caius	283	St. Silverius	536
St. Marcellinus	296	Vigilius	537
St. Marcellus I	308	Pelagius I	556
St. Eusebius	309	John III	561

Benedict I	575	Stephen VI (VII)	896
Pelagius II	579	Romanus	897
St. Gregory the Great	590	Theodore II	897
Sabinian	604	John IX	898
Boniface III	607	Benedict IV	900
St. Boniface IV	608	Leo V	903
St. Deusdedit I	615	Sergius III	904
Boniface V	619	Anastasius III	911
Honorius I	625	Landon	913
Severinus	640	John X	914
John IV	640	Leo VI	928
Theodore I	642	Stephen VII (VIII)	928
St. Martin I	649	John XI	931
St. Eugene I	654	Leo VII	936
St. Vitalian	657	Stephen VIII (IX)	939
Deusdedit II	672	Marinus II	942
Donus	676	Agapitus II	946
St. Agatho	678	John XII	955
St. Leo II	682	Leo VIII	963
St. Benedict II	684	Benedict V	964
John V	685	John XIII	965
Conon	686	Benedict VI	973
St. Sergius I	687	Benedict VII	974
John VI	701	John XIV	983
John VII	705	John XV	985
Sisinnius	708	Gregory V	996
Constantine	708	Silvester II	999
St. Gregory II	715	John XVII	1003
St. Gregory III	731	John XVIII	1004
St. Zachary	741	Sergius IV	1009
Stephen II (III)	752	Benedict VIII	1012
St. Paul, I	757	John XIX	1024
Stephen III (IV)	768	Benedict IX	1032
Adrian I	772	Sylvester III	1045
St. Leo III	795	Benedict IX [2nd term]	1045
Stephen IV (V)	816	Gregory VI	1045
St. Paschal I	817	Clement II	1046
Eugene II	824	Benedict IX [3rd term]	1047
Valentine	827	Damasus II	1048
Gregory IV	827	St Leo IX	1049
Sergius II	844	Victor II	1055
St. Leo IV	847	Stephen X	1057
Benedict III	855	Nicholas II	1059
St. Nicholas the Great	858	Alexander II	1061
Adrian II	867	St. Gregory VII	1073
John VIII	872	B Victor III	1086
Marinus I	882	B Urban II	1088
St. Adrian III	884	Paschal II	1099
Stephen V (VI)	885	Gelasius II	1118
Formosus	891	Callistus II	1119
Boniface VI	896	Honorius II	1124

92

Innocent II	1130	Pius III	1503
Celestine II	1143	Julius II	1503
Lucius II	1144	Leo X	1513
B Eugene III	1145	Adrian VI	1522
Anastasius IV	1153	Clement VII	1523
Adrian IV	1154	Paul III	1534
Alexander III	1159	Julius III	1550
Lucius III	1181	Marcellus II	1555
Urban III	1185	Paul IV	1555
Gregory VIII	1187	Pius IV	1559
Clement III	1187	St. Pius V	1566
Celestine III	1191	Gregory XIII	1572
Innocent III	1198	Sixtus V	1585
Honorius III	1216	Urban VII	1590
Gregory IX	1227	Gregory XIV	1590
Celestine IV	1241	Innocent IX	1591
Innocent IV	1243	Clement VIII	1592
Alexander IV	1254	Leo XI	1605
Urban IV	1261	Paul V	1605
Clement IV	1268	Gregory XV	1621
B Gregory X	1271	Urban VIII	1623
B Innocent V	1276	Innocent X	1644
Adrian V	1276	Alexander VII	1655
John XXI	1276	Clement IX	1667
Nicholas III	1277	Clement X	1670
Martin IV	1281	B Innocent XI	1676
Honorius IV	1285	Alexander VIII	1689
Nicholas IV	1288	Innocent XII	1691
St. Celestine V	1294	Clement XI	1700
Boniface VIII	1294	Innocent XIII	1721
B Benedict XI	1303	Benedict XIII	1724
Clement V	1305	Clement XII	1730
John XXII	1316	Benedict XIV	1740
Benedict XII	1334	Clement XIII	1758
Clement VI	1342	Clement XIV	1769
Innocent VI	1352	Pius VI	1775
B Urban V	1362	Pius VII	1800
Gregory XI	1371	Leo XII	1823
Urban VI	1378	Pius VIII	1829
Boniface IX	1389	Gregory XVI	1831
Innocent VII	1404	Pius IX	1846
Gregory XII	1406	Leo XIII	1878
Martin V	1417	St. Pius X	1903
Eugene IV	1431	Benedict XV	1914
Nicholas V	1447	Pius XI	1922
Callistus III	1455	Pius XII	1939
Pius II	1458	John XXIII	1958
Paul II	1464	Paul VI	1963
Sixtus IV	1471	John Paul I	1978
Innocent VIII	1484	John Paul II	1978
Alexander VI	1492		

Index

95